Design your life; live in abundance

A young person's guide to living a meaningful life

HLELOLWENKHOSI MAMBA

Dedication

. . . .

To my daughter, Ominjalo Ndabezitha:

Baby girl, I want you to know that when I count my blessings, I count you multiple times. You are God's way of showing me how much He loves me.

May you grow to live a meaningful life right from a tender age. May none of your days on Earth be wasted. I love you very much.

Contents

Preface iv

Introduction vii

First things first ... Fear the Lord 1

Get to know yourself 7

A brand called "You" 19

Have a vision for your life 26

Set your goals 31

Do it afraid! 46

Get yourself mentors 53

Use the gift of creative imagination 59

Be an utmost person 65

Sometimes you win, sometimes you learn 75

You don't have time to waste 79

Preface

What do I mean by living in abundance? As I use it in this book, abundance is not about millions in your bank account, owning the latest sleek wheels, or living in a mansion by the beach. You can have all those but still be socially broke, emotionally empty, morally dry, and miserable.

A life of abundance is a potential destiny of all created people, especially those that believe. It is about having a healthy lifestyle in all aspects of your life. A life of abundance is what Apostle John wrote about in 3 John 2 (NKJV), "Beloved, I pray that you may prosper in *all things* and be in health, just as your soul prospers." (Emphasis mine). We all deserve to prosper in *all* things. We ought to be healthy roundabout. Being financially healthy but morally ill makes an imbalanced individual, and that's not a life of abundance.

A healthy spiritual life is foundational to a life of abundance. This is what is described in 3 John 2 as the 'prospering soul'. Our souls should prosper. If the soul prospers, then all the other aspects of life will easily prosper as well. Our soul is the foundation on which all the other parts are built. If this foundation is shaky, then there will be cracks in the rest of the structure of our lives. If this foundation is solid, then our lives will be stable and will stand the test of time.

Our focus during our time together in this book will be on roundabout personal development: socially, academically, financially, and otherwise. Now, all those combined will lead you to a life of overflow, a life of abundance. We are Christians but we live in the world. We don't want to find ourselves being Heavenly-minded until we become earthly irrelevant. We need to be relevant on earth so that the Gospel that we profess will be attractive even to those who are not yet saved. That is important. It is vital that we prosper and thrive in all things, not just speaking in tongues or attending church; not to undermine these, they are important in their own right.

In this book, I advocate for a Christian life that is enjoyable, fulfilling, purposeful, and meaningful. You don't have to be poor and miserable in order for people to believe that you are a true Christian. You don't have to live a substandard life to prove that you are humble. If you do that, you are misrepresenting the God who owns the cattle on a thousand hills (Psalms 50:10), the One who said silver and gold are His (Haggai 2:8).

I will be quick, however, to make it clear that this is not a 'how to get rich' book. It is about how you can live your life with purpose, intention, and a clear vision. That's what I call abundance!

From this book, do not expect any new or 'out of this world' ideas. Rather, the suggestions, as laid out in the following chapters, are really truths that you already 'instinctively' know. The only thing would be that they have been dormant all this while in your life. In this book, I re-arrange the truths so that they are much simpler to apply and live by.

Please note, throughout this book, I will use words like dream, vision, destiny, and purpose to describe the reason for your existence and what you aim to achieve. I use these words interchangeably and to mean the same thing (only for the purpose of this book, otherwise your dictionary will show you that they don't necessarily mean the same thing) because, otherwise using one word in every paragraph throughout the book may make the reading monotonous and boring. Therefore, please take it as if these terms mean the same thing.

Introduction

To some people, life is a nightmare. Yet still, to some, it is a bed of roses. Some people endure life. Yet some still enjoy it. Some people dread the next day of their life because to them it represents a new set of struggles and difficulties. Yet still, some others look forward to the next day because for them it brings a new set of opportunities to advance and enjoy life. These scenarios describe the lives of two groups of people that are alive today. Which group do you belong to? Do you wish tomorrow would never come? Or, do you look forward to the next day with eager anticipation?

This book in your hands is relevant to you, regardless of which group you affiliate with. If you are enjoying life and you have it all together, read on, and get inspired to keep moving forward and possibly soar even higher to the skies above. If you are enduring life, nothing seems to go the way you would like it to, and you feel kind of overwhelmed by life, read on still. This could mark your turning point and bring the revolution you need in your life. Allow me to nudge you to start moving towards enjoying your life.

This book is loaded with suggestions that are meant to help you in your journey of self-development and how you can start living a life you are proud of. If you are willing to put them into practice, your life will be transformed. If not, then you should be OK with me telling you that you are now what you could ever be. I am not asking you to be someone you are not. All I am asking is for you to realize how much dormant and untapped potential lies within you. I encourage you to take advantage of it for the betterment of your life.

Lying inside you is a viable seed of achievement. All it lacks are the necessary conditions for it to germinate. As primary schoolers will tell you, a seed needs oxygen, moisture, and a conducive temperature to germinate. I hope you will find all those conditions in this book, you have the seed in you, and it's viable – that completes the equation.

Right here at the beginning, I want to borrow Paul's words in Philippians 3:13. I also do not consider myself to have taken hold of all that God designed for me to have or become. I am not where I am supposed to be...yet. But I am certain, I am not where I used to be. That's why I thought it right to write to you to share with you the steps I took to get from where I was to where I am. It is my utmost honour and pleasure to do that. Most notably, I will most certainly use the same principles as I outlined here to get to where I know I have to be. I still strive towards that mark daily.

As you might have heard, 'the largest room on earth is the room for improvement.' So, as much as I am glad I am not where I used to be, I acknowledge that the journey ahead of me is still long.

The principles outlined here are a mixture of what life taught me through my journey and the lessons that I have over years gleaned from mentors and the lives of other people who are ahead of me. I am a lifelong student of life. I do promise you that your time spent reading this book will be time well spent, as long as just reading it will not be the end of it. You will then go a step further and practice what I share with you, my highly esteemed friend. Most of it is practical and requires action. I can't think of any other way to help you improve your life apart from encouraging you to be an active participant in your own life. So, that means action, action, and more action. You can't afford to be a bystander and let life happen on its own. Rather, you make life happen for you, by taking an active role and participating in it.

Between you and I, we are in this together!

Let the journey of becoming begin!

1

First things first ... Fear the Lord

The fear of the Lord is the foundation on which a life of abundance is built. It means to hate evil (Prov. 8:13) and to depart from it (Prov. 16:6b).

Here is a promise about it:

> He will be the sure foundation for your times, <u>a rich store of salvation and wisdom and knowledge</u>; the fear of the Lord is the key to this treasure.

> Isaiah 33:6 (NIV)

Wisdom and knowledge are prerequisites for a life of abundance. We are told in the scripture above that God is a rich store for both. The verse further likens wisdom and knowledge to treasure that is locked away. We can only access this treasure through the key, which is the fear of the Lord. It is the master key to all of God's treasures.

Prov. 9:10 says, "The fear of the Lord is the beginning of wisdom." That means once you fear the Lord, you begin to be wise. Now, wisdom is the ability to live life skillfully. The wisdom that comes to you as a result of fearing God enables you to deal wisely in the affairs of life. A wise person does not do things anyhow. His life is neat and organised. We cannot afford to live like mere simple people, not at this time. We ought to depend not only on our natural wisdom but also on the wisdom that God gives us. The nice thing about this kind of wisdom is that none of us can make an excuse for why she doesn't have it. If you know you lack wisdom, as evidenced by the decisions and choices you make for your life, don't hesitate to ask for it from the Lord. He will definitely give it to you, not just a small portion, but He will give it to you liberally, for He knows how important it is for you to have it.

> If any of you lacks wisdom, let him ask of God, who gives to all *liberally* and without reproach, and it will be given to him.
>
> James 1:5 (NKJV)

You need this wisdom to build a meaningful life for yourself— a life that will bring glory to God. Without wisdom, a lot is at stake. Our lives are built primarily by the choices and decisions that we make every day. If we have wisdom, that will be reflected in the kind of choices and decisions that we make, and that's what will build our lives.

Prov. 1:7 (NKJV) says, "The fear of the Lord is the beginning of knowledge." That means if you fear the Lord, you begin to be knowledgeable about certain things that many people are ignorant about. It is because of this ignorance that those people are not living in abundance.

Ps. 25:14-15 (NKJV) says, "The secret of the Lord is with those who fear Him. He will show them His covenant." If anything is a secret, then only a select few know about it. There are success secrets that the Lord only reveals to those who fear Him. I mean the success that leads to abundance accumulated only through clean and above reproach methods.

We have been deceived into believing that for one to be successful, they need to be involved in some shady dealings and bribes here and there. That's a lie from the pit of hell. This is the very same lie that has made Christians accept a substandard life because Christian teachings forbid these kinds of practises. So, because Christians are not supposed to bribe anyone and they should do everything by the book, they think they can't live in abundance. I will repeat: that is a lie from the pit of hell. You can live a life of abundance without bending or breaking any laws, as long as you have the key to God's treasure box—the fear of the Lord. This key will give you access to wisdom and knowledge —the treasure in there.

Ps. 25:15 goes on to say, " ...He will show them His covenant." Which covenant? You must be asking. Remember that God made a covenant of abundance with Abraham. He further went on to promise that it would be a generational covenant that would not only be enjoyed by Abraham alone but also by the generations after him—his seed. According to the scriptures, we are the seed of Abraham, and because of that, we are also partakers in this covenant.

In Gen.13:2, we read that Abram was a man of abundance. I am not only talking about spiritual abundance but also material possessions. Abram had livestock, silver, and gold. One thing about Abram, who later became Abraham, was that he feared the Lord. As such, he had access to God's secrets of success. Gen. 18:17 says, and the Lord said, "Shall I hide from Abraham what I am doing?" There are things that God will fail to hide from you if you fear Him, that He will hide from others. His secret will be with you.

Isaac, Abraham's son, took part in the covenant. Of him, we read in Gen. 26:12–14 that he was a man of abundance as well. He had possessions of flocks, herds, and servants. What makes Isaac's story even sweeter is the fact that he lived in abundance in a land of famine where no one thought abundance was possible. This goes to show that abundance is possible wherever you are, as long as you are operating under the blessing of the covenant as a seed of Abraham. Geographical location should not be a limiting factor.

After Isaac, there was Jacob, and we read a similar story about him as well in Gen. 30:43. Jacob was working for his uncle Laban, tending his flocks. Still, with that kind of job, Jacob became exceedingly prosperous and had large flocks of his own and servants. That's abundance.

From Jacob's story, we learn that you don't necessarily need to have a white-collar job in order to live a life of abundance. You can be doing the kind of job that everyone despises, like being a herdsman, but if you are under the covenantal blessing, then that's what will make all the difference.

Lastly, in Gen. 39:2–3, we read an account of Joseph's story. We are told that he was a successful man. All that he did prospered. The main reason behind Joseph's success was the fact that the Lord was with him. Remember that Joseph was a slave in a foreign land. Regardless of that, he still lived in abundance. From his story, we learn that you may not be in your home country, but as long as you are under the covenant, the Lord will be with you and you will flourish in that foreign land.

Joseph feared the Lord. He hated evil, and he fled from it. Remember when Potiphar's wife presented him with an opportunity to lie with her? He asked her how he could commit such wickedness and sin against God. Joseph displayed utmost fear and reverence for the Lord. No wonder the Lord blessed him abundantly. He would have just taken the offer, and no one would have known about it except the two of them. But his fear of the Lord deterred him from doing it.

The stories of these men should reassure us that no matter who you are, where you are, or what kind of job you do, a life of abundance is, beyond any shadow of doubt, your portion. Your only responsibility should be to ensure that you fear the Lord; that is what unlocks everything you can ever need for a life of abundance.

Let us look at this verse in Ps. 103:7 (NKJV):

> He made known His ways to Moses, His acts to the children of Israel.

God revealed His ways to Moses, but to the rest of the children of Israel, He only showed them His acts. If you fear the Lord, you are not going to stop at just seeing His works, you will also know His ways. If you don't fear the Lord, you will end at knowing that God enables people to live in abundance, but you will never enjoy the abundance yourself. If you fear the Lord, He will give you His secret recipe for abundance.

If you only know the works of God, you are like someone who knows the answer to a mathematical problem but doesn't know the formula used to solve that particular problem. If you know His way, then you know step-by-step the formula for solving the problem. If we had made the fear of the Lord our way of life, there are a lot of things we would have done differently as guided by His wise counsel.

The fear of the Lord is the fountain of life (Prov. 14:27), and it prolongs days (Prov. 10:27). These are wonderful news. So, if you fear the Lord, He will not only give you access to abundance, but He will also make you escape the snares of death so that you live long enough to enjoy your abundance to the fullest. So, basically, the fear of the Lord is a full package.

Pursue the fear of the Lord with all that you have. If you want knowledge, fear God. If you want wisdom, fear God. If you fear Him, you will seek Him, and if you seek Him, you will never lack any good thing (Ps. 34:10, NKJV). There is no want for those who fear Him (Ps. 34:9, NKJV). If you have no want, then you are in a life of abundance!

2

Get to know yourself

Many people go through life without taking the time to ask the question, "Who am I?", confronting themselves and taking the time to discover what makes them as individuals. It is for this reason that these people never get to live out their lives to their full potential. They don't know what they are capable of doing because they never take the time to study themselves. Some live up to what other people describe them to be, no matter how limiting it is. To them, the next person's opinion of who they are is the gospel truth, because they have no other to compare it with. They don't have their own opinion of who they are, so they rely on external opinions. Some, because they don't know who they are and how valuable they are, conduct themselves anyhow – handling themselves like a cheap piece of cloth, absolutely without any worth.

When asked the question, "Who are you?", The first responses many people give are usually their age, their ethnic background, or the position they hold in their workplace. This is how most of us have been programmed – to look at ourselves through the lenses of the titles we hold or the labels that life has given us. If you don't have prestigious and fancy titles, then you are tempted to think that those who do are better than you.

Often, what other people describe you as is not what you really are. Their description of your person is based solely on what they have observed in a few hours, or maybe a couple of months, or the years they have spent with you. But that's not enough time to draw conclusions. If you don't describe yourself – who you are and what you can do – then the people around you will not think twice about doing it for you. If you don't make a series of "I" statements, then you have to be comfortable living with a series of "you" statements. In spite of what they are.

You need to shift your focus away from the descriptions of the outside to your inward self – at your very core. If you accept people's descriptions of who you are and what you can do, you will never know how amazing, gifted, and talented you are. Entertaining people's opinions of you is a recipe for frustration and depression. At best, people's opinions may allow you to function, but they will still deprive you of your fulfillment and satisfaction. They are not likely to propel you to reach your full potential. Oprah Winfrey once said, "Often we don't realize who we are meant to be because we are so busy trying to live up someone else's ideas."

I have taken time to observe the lives of some great people of our time. For most of them, I discovered that there were several "you" statements that were made to them that they have, through their lives, falsified. These great men and women didn't just prove these statements otherwise. It was possible for them to do it because when the "you" statements came, they had no place in their lives because they were already loaded with "I" statements. Below, I give you examples of such individuals.

Lisa Nichols, an African American woman, was told by her teacher that she was a terrible English writer and the worst speaker she had ever met. Lisa says the highest grade she ever got in school was a C+. As such, her public speaking teacher suggested to her that she never speak in public. Today, Lisa is the author of several bestselling books and a sought-after conference speaker who speaks at conferences with thousands at a time around the globe. She is a multimillionaire in U.S. dollars and one of the few black women in America to own a public company. Had she believed and bent under the heavy weight of her teacher's analysis and description of her, what do you think would have become of her?

Les Brown, while still in school, was told that he was mentally retarded and would never achieve much in life. When he tells his story, he says he was born on the floor of one of America's poorest neighbourhoods. He says he was deserted while still a baby and was rescued by a single woman who had adopted him along with seven other kids. This woman had barely enough to feed and clothe all the kids because she got her income working as a cleaner. She fed them from the leftovers she would collect from the homes she worked for. Today, Les is a businessman, a world-renowned speaker, and the author of several books. He is also a multimillionaire, and he travels the world.

There are many others like them, even in Africa and Swaziland, but I will stop here and ask you, "What do you think helped them achieve this greatness?" Maybe it was true that Lisa was a terrible writer and speaker. Probably Les was actually mentally retarded. But today, can anyone tell these were once their stories? Certainly not. This goes to show that your story today doesn't have to be your story tomorrow. It is within your ability to change your story.

The "you" statements made to them had no place in them because they had "I" statements that preoccupied their being. "I" statements are and will always be more powerful than "you" statements. You should ensure that your "I" statements are positive and affirming to you. Don't make demeaning statements that will suck all the vitality out of you, cripple your energies, and hinder you from becoming the wonder youngster that you can be.

Avoid making your "I" statements at times when you are experiencing your lowest points or setbacks. If you have to, try to make statements that describe what you want to become of the situation and not what the current moment looks like. For example, if you just flopped a class, don't make statements like, "I am such an idiot." "I am dumb." "I am incapable." Such statements will send you into a downward spiral, and you might not recover from it. In the face of such situations, you can affirm yourself with statements such as, "I can do this." "I am capable." You need to be your own cheerleader and fan. Be your favourite person.

This reminds me of my first year at the university as an undergraduate. I was enrolled in the faculty of science. During the application process, people would ask me what programme I was applying for. I would tell them, "Bachelor of Science." In reaction, their faces would turn pale (well, I mean that figuratively). They would exclaim, "Science?" "Why on earth did you choose science?" Then they would go on and on about how challenging the programme is, giving me an account of some people who struggled even to the point of dropping out or being discontinued from it. Basically, they were telling me that I don't have what it takes to be a science major. Well, for a moment, such conversations would get me thinking, cause me to doubt myself, and even make me think of reconsidering my choice. However, I managed to keep my cool and didn't change my programme.

The first semester started. I tried so hard to be on top of my game, but I was already polluted by those "you" statements from my conversations. The first test came; it was for one of my mathematics courses. I studied so hard. On the last night, when the test was to be written the following morning, I slept for about three hours because it was my last opportunity to absorb as much as I could before I sat for the test. Yes! The test scripts were returned two weeks later. Mine had a ten percent on it. I couldn't believe my eyes. After so many hours of studying. It felt like a dream, except that I was not on my bed. One of my classmates who happened to see my score as I received my paper came to me and said, "You see, because you have started with such a score. You better get ready to retake the course next year. I'm talking from experience. I'm taking this class for the second time because this is what happened to me too." This was a reality check for me. I remembered all those conversations I had had before school began. It would seem those people were right after all. I had misjudged my abilities. I shouldn't have chosen a science course. I had hit rock bottom, and I was doomed.

As these thoughts went through my mind, I was slowly sinking into despair. My future started fading. For a moment, I lost all courage to go on. I was ready to quit. Thank God it was a Friday. I went straight to my dormitory and cried myself to sleep. I woke up with a heavy soul. I was asking myself, if all the effort I had put into preparing for this test was worth only ten percent, what else could I do? I had done all I thought there was to do. I came up with a solution. The people I had spoken to, those who thought I didn't have what it takes to study a science course, had suggested another non-scientific course that I could take. I thought to myself, "If they were right about science being impossible for me, then they must have been right about that other course they suggested." I was ready to switch courses and was seriously considering it.

It wasn't until I was back to my senses that I made statements that countered those I had previously made when I received my script. I affirmed myself. I assured myself I was capable and that this was just a minor setback that I could rectify. I was very right, because I did. Four years later, I graduated with my Bachelor of Science degree and was among the best-performing students in my class. What would have become of me had I switched those courses? Today, I would be stuck with a resort qualification I am not passionate about. All my success in that resort career would still leave me with a void that would lead to frustration.

Les Brown once said, "Someone's opinion of you does not have to become your reality." I can't agree more with this truth. But if you don't have an opinion to contradict the opinions others have about you, then their opinion will definitely be your reality. How sad if it is a twisted one.

Can you imagine if Lisa didn't have an opinion about herself becoming an author? Then her teacher's opinion of her being a terrible writer would have proven true. Obviously, she wouldn't be enjoying the success she's enjoying today. The lesson here is that if you allow other people's opinions of you to matter and take precedence in your life, you will have crippled energies and contracted abilities. Walter Bagehot said, "The greatest pleasure in life is doing what other people say you cannot do." When you break the ceiling that people have set for you and supersede their expectations of you, then you sure should be proud of yourself. Enjoy seeing their mouth drop open when they look at you in disbelief at how wrong they were to undermine you like that.

Let's look at how you can develop a positive and healthy opinion of yourself.

Ask the key question

The starting point would be asking yourself the key question, "Who am I?" There are many facets to the answer to this question. I will consider as many of them as possible.

Asking yourself this question is the first step towards your self-assessment, or self-study. This is where you explore yourself to the fullest. You are not going to become who you really are until you give yourself permission to do so, after you have learned what that looks like. The only way to learn who you are is through self-study.

Sit down, if need be, in a quiet place and take a tour of yourself. As you do this self-study, be honest with yourself. If you give a "half-cooked" answer to this question, you will not be deceiving anyone else but yourself. That is why you need to carefully think the question through before you respond. There is no rush to give an answer! It's not like someone has a gun to your head demanding an answer as in yesterday.

Take this as your opportunity to get to know yourself better, something you might not have seen the need for before this time, but believe me, it is very important that you do it. An honest and diligent self-assessment will help you discover your likes and dislikes, strengths and weaknesses, fears, interests, and other qualities that you might have but may not be aware of. It is vital for you to know all these things about yourself if you are working on designing a life of abundance.

A proper self-assessment helps you build up your self-concept. A self-concept is the idea you hold of yourself as made up of the beliefs that you have about yourself. What do you believe about yourself? This is your identity.

The self-assessment stage is the most important, and I really cannot overstate its importance. A proper and rich self-assessment helps you come up with a very strong, positive, and healthy self-concept or self-identity. With these, you are unstoppable. A poor self-assessment leads to an identity crisis. This result occurs when you fail to understand yourself. You become uncertain of who you are and what you can do. Thus, everything else around you becomes confusing. There is a thin line between positive self-identity and negative self-identity (or identity crisis). I have seen people who I thought had a healthy, positive self-identity suddenly crash into an identity crisis. I call this thin line "identity theft". This is orchestrated by the master thief and no one else. The Bible says in John 10:10 that he comes only to steal, kill, and destroy.

Let's make an example of identity theft. Let's say I have a beautiful and brilliant teenage schoolgirl. She is well respected among her peers at school because she has both beauty and brains. This boosts her self-esteem and gives her a positive self-identity. Then she makes one mistake. She falls pregnant, and she's forced to drop out of school. The father of her child deserts her and does not take responsibility for his child. Her parents neglect her because they are too disappointed by her actions. She struggles to support the baby by herself. She can't take care of herself, and she becomes a sorry sight.

She sees some of her peers (who were not as brilliant as she was) graduate from high school and get accepted into college. She becomes ashamed of herself; she feels like a failure; she looks like one; and eventually she develops negative self-esteem.

This is the same person who had everything going well for her. Not long ago, she had it all together. Now, she has allowed just one event in her life to ruin every good thing she had.

It is very important to guard against identity theft. There are many things that make people victims of identity theft, but that's beyond the scope of this book. I will, however, suggest ways of dealing with setbacks to avoid identity crises in the coming chapters. And if that leaves you yearning for more, then may I recommend that you get my other book, "Life's Interruptions: Surviving Setbacks and Bouncing Back like a Tennis Ball."

From your self-concept, you can now come up with your self-image. Self-image is about the mental picture that you have of yourself. This is the same picture that you want people to see when they look at you. As such, many people have what I would like to call a "chameleon" self-image. They paint different pictures of themselves depending on where they are. Each picture is designed to suit the environment she or he is in at that particular time. This is very close to an identity crisis, where the individual has genuine difficulty understanding who he really is.

Stacey Speller, in her book, *The Designer Life*, puts it this way: she says, "There is the authentic you, and then there is the representative you." People with a chameleon self-image have different masks they put on over their authentic selves each time they want to make an impression. In church, they wear this innocent, born-again mask to impress the church leader or the Pastor. When with friends, they wear this crazy wild animal mask to impress them. If you do this, you must know that you are not deceiving anyone but yourself. You owe it to yourself to be true to yourself at all times. Do not wear masks to make an impression or to try to impress people. You can't enjoy life if you are still playing this hide-and-seek game.

It has been said that life is a game that you have to play, but this is not how we play this game called life. If you decide to play it this way, if you win the game, you lose your life because this is just self-deception and living a lie. Pretending to be someone you are not deprives you of the opportunity to live your authentic life and enjoy who you are.

It is important that you pay special attention and be very cautious about how you design your self-image because it will in turn set boundaries for your performance in life. You cannot outperform your self-image. It is important to note that you are not born with your self-image. You formulate it along the way as you grow, and you are 100 percent responsible for it. If it's a faulty negative one, you have no one else to blame but yourself.

Developing a healthy self-image is a must if you are to live a successful life and make a difference. If your life could be likened to a car, your self-image would be the cruise control in that car. In any car, the role of cruise control is to maintain the speed at which the car travels, as set by the driver. If this mechanism is set at 100 km/h, that's the speed the car will maintain. It will change only slightly; speeding up a little as it goes downhill or slowing down a little as it encounters steep slopes. After this, the car will go back to the 100 km/h programmed in the speed or cruise control.

Your self-image operates under similar principles as the cruise control in a car. If you exceed the bounderies of your achievements, as set by your self-image, and go even a little beyond them, your self-image will pull you back to what is "normal" for you. This means that you will never rise above the image you have of yourself in your mind. If all you "see" of yourself is being an employee in a company owned by someone else, then your self-image will not allow you to be an employer in your own company. It doesn't allow you to be an overachiever. The good thing about it, though, is that if you underperform, your self-image will pull you back up. This is why it is imperative that you develop a healthy, positive one. A healthy self-image will force you to achieve your goals against all odds. If your self-image has made you believe that you are worth more, it will also help you reach for and enjoy it.

You develop your self-image in one of three ways. It may stem from the beliefs you have about yourself (this should be the case), it may be a result of how your parents regarded you, or it may be what other people, including your peers, say about you. This is why you need to do a thorough self-assessment, because if you have done your self-assessment well, then you will know who you are. Another person's opinion of you becomes immaterial, especially if it is negative. A trap you can't escape is the negative opinion you have about yourself. This one will make you your own prisoner because you take it with you wherever you go. Having explored yourself and discovered who you are, the finished product of your self-assessment is what I would like to call a brand called "You".

3

A brand called "You"

A brand is used in business circles. This is about a type of product associated with a particular company. Different companies have different brands that identify them. I want to borrow this concept from the business world to make a certain point. Out of the millions of companies in the world, each has its own brand, and all these brands are different from each other. There are good and bad brands. But what makes a good brand? Let's explore a few characteristics that distinguish a brand and make it stand out from the rest.

A good brand has a purpose.

Before a company starts the design of its brand, it should first have a purpose for the brand. This purpose can be to show potential customers what the company does or anything else the company's management deems fit. You are your own brand, and you are the manager of this brand called "you." As such, it is your responsibility to come up with a purpose for this brand. Your purpose should be the answers to the questions, "Why do I exist?" and "What am I about on this earth?"

If you see the brand of the Coca-Cola Company, you can immediately attach purpose to it, right? What would that purpose be? Maybe to produce drinks to quench thirst. Right? If you see the brand "T.D. Jakes" what purpose would you attach? I guess you answered, "To preach the gospel." What if you see the brand "Bill Gates"? What purpose would you attach it to? To make more money each day, right? After all he's one of the leading businessmen in the world, so that would make sense. Now, what purpose can be attached to the brand called "you"? Purpose is what keeps you alive. It is what you need to do before your days on earth come to an end.

Dr. Myles Munroe once said, "The greatest tragedy in life is not the death of a loved one; the greatest tragedy in life is life without a purpose." Surely, you don't want to be a victim of this tragedy. It is only when you discover your purpose that you start living; until then, you are only existing. For many people, the tragedy is not that life ends too soon; it is that they wait too long to begin it. So don't wait until it is too late. More on purpose in the coming chapters.

A good brand has high value.

Every company strives to ensure that its brand has the highest value among its competitors in the market. As an individual, you must also value yourself. How much value people will attach to you will depend on how much value you attach to yourself. You cannot expect people to treat you with honour and respect if you live a low and irresponsible life. You should give the people around you a reason to respect you by the way you conduct yourself.

If, as a girl, you stoop so low and live a "loose life", hooking up with every male that smiles at you, then you don't have much value. Good brands are pricey; they produce high-quality products, and not everyone can afford them. As a young man who attaches high value to himself, not everything in a skirt qualifies to be your girlfriend and eventually your wife; only those that have set themselves apart and are in your league. This is not to say you should look down on people or be arrogant. It only means know your worth.

While I was still in school, I valued myself so highly. I told myself I would not date any boy until I was ready to date with the intention of marrying that individual. I thought I was very beautiful, at least to myself if not to everyone else. As such, any boy who would have me for a girlfriend should be eternally grateful because I was a rare find. I esteemed myself so highly that I thought I would not give any boy the satisfaction of dating me. I was friendly to as many of my male schoolmates as they would want to befriend me. But that is how far I was willing to go—to mere friendship. I didn't have a bosom male friend because I didn't want to compromise and make myself vulnerable. What if I developed feelings for him? Because that happens if boys and girls become very close to each other. In the event these male friends misread the whole friendship thing and thought I was interested in them and would start pursuing me, hell would break loose. I would cut off all communication with them. That's how much I valued myself as a teenager. The value of a brand is shown by how hard the company strives to protect and defend it.

A good brand has a good reputation.

Every brand out there is associated with some kind of reputation. Every company ensures its brand has a good reputation. It can build its reputation through the prompt delivery of its goods or services, excellent customer service, or being the manufacture of high-quality products. There is nothing as demeaning in the life of a young person as a bad reputation.

Reputation is built and earned. It is a choice to build a good reputation and become a respectable young man or woman. Everyone likes to be associated with an individual with a good reputation. As a young person, you are at a critical stage where you are still designing your life and trying to figure out what you want out of life. You will need people at some point in time to help you on this journey. It will be easier for people to help you if you are reputable. No one would want to associate with you if you were always on the police's most wanted list. Make sure you build a good reputation for yourself. This will also boost your self-confidence and make it easier for you to relate to different people.

A good brand is different and unique.

The differences among brands are what make each of them stand out among the others in competition. A good brand is authentic and original. It is not an imitation of any other. It is good and advisable to have role models and mentors—people who are several steps ahead of you who you look up to and learn from. It is wrong, however, to become a "carbon copy" of your mentor. When you do that, you must know that you have limited yourself.

It has been said that if you imitate someone else, the best you can be is second-best because you cannot outdo the person you are imitating. Role models and mentors are before you as a source of inspiration, not to be imitated. Be original, different, and unique. Some people fall into the temptation of admiring their mentors to the extent of dressing and even speaking like them. When you do that, just know that you have limited yourself and your creativity. I dare you to be different. This brand called "you" was created by God. He created you as a champion and a genius. You have been marked by majesty and fashioned by divinity. You are someone incredibly special and undeniably unique. You are priceless, and you better embrace that because it's true!

A good brand is dynamic.

The market is dynamic, and it changes all the time. Brand managers should keep up with the times to prevent being outcompeted. They should always keep their fingers on the pulse of the market and upgrade or improve their brand according to the changes in the market. You are your own brand manager. It is therefore your responsibility to upgrade yourself as frequently as possible. For example, you can't relax in this day and age relax after graduating with a diploma. Go ahead and do your bachelor's degree, then your master's degree, all the way to your PhD as opportunity allows. Don't just rest on your laurels because you have a paper that you think can allow you to start job hunting. Keep upgrading yourself and adding value to yourself. Take some short courses occasionally to enhance your main degree. This will help you be more qualified for the job you are hoping for. It will give you a competitive advantage over other people with whom you are vying for the same position. Above all else, it will make you competent in your work.

There are many ways to add value to and improve your brand. You can learn a new skill (whether it be cooking, driving, singing, etc.) or hone your talent. You can attend a few classes and graduate. When you add value to your life, you are making yourself more useful to the people around you. You may find that they are forced to start paying you for what you have added in your life. If you have learned to cook, people may ask you to be the supplier of food for their events and pay you for your services. If you have learned to sing, you may be hired to sing at big events and cash in because of that skill.

Adding value may also be about honing your talent. Raw talent is usually not good enough. This is because many people out there are as talented as you are. Make yourself a cut above the rest and a rare find by polishing up your talent. You can do this by getting a coach with the same talent and more experience, or you can just go to someone who can actually teach you in a formal setting like a class. When you are rare, people will come find you. Remember, people dig for gold and they dive for pearls, but nobody pays attention to the stones that are found scattered everywhere.

You can be a talented musician, but your talent alone will not help you secure gigs. This is because there are many other talented musicians out there. But if you enrol in a music school where you will be taught ways to spice up your talent, then you will have put yourself in a better position and will be more likely to lend gigs where you will get paid well. Life has become very competitive, so you should always make sure that you invest in yourself so you can beat the competition. The world is a dynamic place, and only dynamic people survive. If you are not dynamic, you will be overwhelmed, frustrated, and outcompeted in the process.

4

Have a vision for your life

••••••••••••••••••••••••••••••••••••••

Probably by now you have heard several definitions of the word "vision". Allow me to add one more to your collection of definitions. A vision is a dream that you have while wide awake. It is that dream that you have while wide awake that eventually comes to pass.

A vision is the result of creative dreaming about your future. Where dreaming about your future is concerned, don't be intimidated by anything. Entertain those disruptive and innovative imaginations that will make you uncomfortable where you are in this present moment. Allow yourself to be comfortable with being uncomfortable; that's the only time you can be in a better position to alter your status quo and get on the path towards your vision and dream.

A vision allows you to finish before you begin. It helps you define what you, as an individual, want to achieve in your lifetime. Just like no one can build a house without first having an idea of what the finished structure should look like, as depicted in the house plan, you also cannot achieve a meaningful future without a vision; that's the blueprint for your life. Hellen Keller was blind, and she was asked what she considered to be the worst thing than not having sight. This was her response: "The worst thing than not having sight is having sight without vision."

A vision is what you need to help you live on purpose and experience abundance in life. I have already referred to Dr. Myles Munroe's definition of tragedy as "life without purpose." If you do not have a vision for your life, then you live by default. You take whatever life throws at you. You become a victim of life, and you let life happen. But if you have a vision, you don't live by default. You live on purpose. You don't let life happen; you make it happen. You are not a victim of life; you are a victor in life.

You must be aware that life will not give you what you deserve, but what you demand from it. Life is not good at judging your worth so as to give you what matches your value. Usually, life gives you the exact opposite of what you deserve. Ever heard of people asking, "Why do bad things always happen to good people?" Yes, that's life! If you allow it, it will give you what you least expect, and most of the time, it won't be good. You've got to make it give you what you think and believe is due to you. You cannot demand anything from life if you don't have a vision. It is your vision that will give you an idea of what you want and need from life.

No one deserves to be a victim in life, but many people are because they didn't demand anything out of life. Life dealt them anything, they accepted it, and they have to live with it. As Neale Donald Walsch once wrote; "Do not search for life's meaning, give it meaning. Then announce and declare who you choose to be." Until you declare who you are or who you want to be, then life will not think twice about defining you. If you are going to sit there and look cute, trying to make sense out of life, I bet you are not likely to find it. Life doesn't have meaning until you give it one. The only way to give it meaning is to have a clear vision, and then your life will start to make a whole lot of sense. Until then, you will always find life confusing and unsatisfying.

You will never start living until you have a vision. The closest you can get to living is to exist. Before you know it, you will be at the end of your life. You won't quite clearly remember how your life started, and the end will catch you by surprise because you did not have a picture of how you wanted to live it and then how you would like it to end. So, it will end anyhow, and in the process, it will catch you off guard.

As I have already said, for many people, the tragedy is not that life ends too soon. It is that they waited too long to begin it. Once again, Dr. Myles Munroe once said, "The richest place on earth is not the gold or diamond mines, nor is it the oil reserves. Rather, it is the cemetery. Because buried there are dreams that were never fulfilled, songs that were never sung, and books that were never written." When you die, you don't want to add to the "underground wealth." Now, do you? It would be a waste since no one would have access to that wealth anymore. No one can take advantage of it and enjoy it. The fact that you are reading this book and that you have read it this far speaks volumes about your desire to make life happen. I pray so hard that in it you find the answers you are looking for and that it may give you the encouragement you need to pursue life intentionally and with a purpose.

I am not trying to scare you with death. The truth is, one day all of us will die. However, the way we die will differ from individual to individual. For some people death, catches them unaware, while for others, they prepare for it. The best way you can prepare for your death is to make every single day of your life count; and live your life to the fullest. Be diligent in life. The book of Ecclesiastes instructs us to do with all our might everything that our hands find to do. You have to use all the energy you have to design your life this side of the grave. Don't reserve any, because in the grave and beyond, none of it will be useful. If you were to die today, you would never again have the opportunity to use that energy that's still untapped. There is no such thing in your life as an unimportant day. Each day brings you a new set of possibilities and opportunities, and it deserves your undivided attention so that you can make the most of it.

Habakkuk 2:2 (NKJV) says, "Write the vision and make it plain on tablets..." Having a vision is the first step. The second step is to write the vision down. This is very important because it will help you remember your vision. Do not entrust this great responsibility to your memory, lest you lose it. Don't just write it and then tuck it away; keep it within your sight. You've probably heard people say, "Out of sight, out of mind." Once your vision is out of your mind, you are not likely to make it happen. I remember back in the days when I wrote my dreams on a piece of paper and lost it. I couldn't remember what I had written on that piece of paper, and ten years later, when the paper resurfaced, none of the things I had written had come to pass.

Having a vision is one thing. Writing it down is another, and it is the first step towards achieving it. Keeping the written vision in a place where your eyes can constantly see it increases the chances of your vision being fulfilled. If possible, you can even have your vision in colourful pictures. Paste these pictures on a cork board to make your vision board or anywhere that you will see them when you wake up in the morning and before you go to bed at night. You can also paste the pictures in an exercise book to make a vision book. Do whatever suits you best, as long as the end result is your colorful vision painted before your eyes. Having your vision within your sight will keep you focused and motivated to achieve it.

Your vision is a complete picture of your life that you aim to "paint" during a specified period. The building blocks of your vision are your goals. Putting together those goals will give you a completed "structure," the vision. In the next chapter, I will discuss more on goals.

5

Set your goals

···

Some of us have big visions. Looking at the vision as a whole can be overwhelming. Sometimes you can even become discouraged and feel like you don't have what it takes to build up that vision. This is why, therefore, it becomes very important that you break down your vision into smaller "chunks" that are not as overwhelming, smaller pieces that you can handle, one piece at a time. These small chunks are what I call "goals".

Don't think of goals as something complicated and out of this world. They are simply your wishes put into actionable words. As such, you should make them simple, clear, and easy to understand. Tackle one goal at a time. Each of these goals is like a step on a ladder. As you achieve it, you are a step closer to your bigger picture, your vision. As you achieve one goal after another, you will see your vision slowly taking shape. That's reason enough to be excited and proud of yourself.

Any journey you can ever take in your life, no matter how long it is, starts with a single step in the right direction. The first goal you achieve will be the first step in the journey towards achieving your dream.

You can also think of it as a puzzle, if that makes more sense to you. Each goal represents a piece of the puzzle. It's extremely difficult—close to impossible—to put each piece in its rightful place if you have no idea what the complete picture should look like. That is why, for every puzzle, the picture you are supposed to put together is always shown before you start. As you put each piece in place, you are slowly building towards the finished product. In this case, your vision is the completed picture. You can't have goals if you don't have a vision. It is your vision that will determine what goals you can set and which goals have to be attended to first.

You have been given the opportunity to create a masterpiece out of your life. Your goals are the raw materials that will make up this work of art that everyone will admire at the end. Weave these goals together to produce your vision. Each day, ensure that your goals are still aligned with the bigger picture of your vision. Aim at each goal until you achieve it, then move on to the next one. Your abundance begins the moment you start achieving the first goal. Every other day should be another day to achieve another goal.

It has been said that what gets celebrated gets repeated. Therefore, celebrate each goal as you achieve it. Celebrating that micro win will renew your courage, get you all cranked up, and keep you enthusiastic to forge on towards the macro win —when you finally make your vision a reality. Don't wait until you have the entire vision accomplished to celebrate. Waiting that long will drain vitality out of you. You need to keep yourself motivated to keep going forward in spite of any setbacks that you may have to deal with.

Michael Hyatt, an expert on goal setting, teaches that there are three zones in which one can set goals: *the comfort zone, the discomfort zone*, and *the delusional zone*.

He says the comfort zone is where you set safe goals that will cost you nothing to achieve. You invest little to no effort to achieve your goals in this zone. Where your goals are concerned, you can be passive but still achieve them.

Goals set in the discomfort zone can give you sleepless nights. They will stretch you to your limits. They demand that you take an active role in order for you to achieve them; otherwise, they will not see the light of day.

You need to set your goals in both of these zones. Don't just set goals in the discomfort zone, because then all your goals will be labour-intensive and may end up getting you burned out. You need those easy-to-achieve goals that you will achieve with minimal effort to get motivated to tackle the more demanding ones.

Goals set in the delusional zone are not different from self-deception. These are the goals you cannot achieve even once in a blue moon. When you set your goals in this zone, you are setting yourself up for disappointment and dismal failure. An example would be an absurd goal such as "*I want to build my mansion deep in the ocean.*" Of course, this may be a bit extreme for an example, but you get the picture.

Goals are not just mere statements that tell you what to do. They are also like your guard rails. They keep you from wandering away from the path leading to your vision, ensuring that you are always aiming at the bull's eye.

As I note below, your goals should be measurable. And after you have set them, you will need to put in place indicators and milestones that you will use to assess progress. These will help you measure the achievement of your goals. The indicators will be your early warnings to signal deviations from your goals. You need these to stay on course. Otherwise, you might not hit the bull's eye as you intended. Your vision should remain your point of reference. Your indicators are indispensable for the evaluation and monitoring of progress in the trajectory of your vision.

Goals that will be accomplished have specific characteristics. I have learned the art of goal-setting from different life coaches. Most of them will tell you that you have to set S.M.A.R.T. goals. As you may already know, S.M.A.R.T. is an acronym that means S: specific, M: measurable, A: achievable, R: realistic, and T: time-bound. I will use the same principles but word them slightly differently.

When setting goals that you intend to achieve, you have to answer the five 'wh-'questions: what, why, when, where, and how. Let's take a moment to look at each of these questions.

What?

Your goals should answer the question, "*What do I want to do?*" For goals that will be achieved, the answer to this question should not be vague and leave one guessing what message you were trying to convey. It should be a specific answer that leaves no room for doubt and confusion. In addition to the key question, "What do you want to do?" other supporting and equally important questions are, *"What obstacles do I have to overcome in order to achieve what I aim to achieve?" "What set of skills will I need to achieve what I am aiming for?"*

Basically, these are asking you to sit down and calculate the costs of achieving this vision. Answering them will help you determine if you are ready to go on this fascinating adventure of achieving your vision. Jesus taught us how to do this neatly in Luke 14:28-33. He spoke about how a person intending to build a tower should first sit down and estimate the cost to see if he has enough money to complete it.

According to this passage of scripture, the first thing to do is to *sit down*. Once you have your vision, a clear picture of what you want to do, and a clear image of your desired destiny, sit down. This doesn't mean you should sit down and snooze. It simply means stop, don't rush, get quiet, get away from noise and distraction, and think. Think hard and long if necessary. At times, we get so busy doing things that aren't going to profit us much. We get so busy that by the time we realise that what we are doing is not worth it, we are already exhausted.

Next, Jesus said to *estimate*. This means you have to use your mind to imagine and analyse what has to be done. Don't just fumble into it. Stop, think, and count. Go into it with your head up and your eyes wide open. On estimating the cost, you may find that these costs include reducing your sleeping hours and extending the hours you work on your vision. Sometimes your vision may cost you your friends, especially if they do not add any value but rather block the path to your vision. Estimate and make sure you have everything in place to complete the journey. You don't want to start something that you will not finish.

Sometimes it helps to look at your costs from a different angle. Looking at them in light of what you may need to sacrifice in order to achieve your dream may get you discouraged, especially if you consider those costs too high. To avoid getting overwhelmed by what it may cost you to get to your dream, you may look at it from the perspective of what it will cost you not to get there. Imagine what your dream will do for you if you achieve it.

If you dream of owning a business, realising that dream will make you your own boss. It will stop you from living from paycheck to paycheck. It will afford you financial freedom. It will help increase your net worth and even allow you to make a difference in the lives of others by donating to charity organisations. Failure to work on your dream would mean you deprive yourself of the opportunity to enjoy all these. It would cost you your happiness, and you would live a life you were not satisfied with or even proud of. Until you are ready to work on your vision, you will have to be OK with paying this cost. If you are not, then you will show it by doing something about working on your vision.

Carefully considering what you will become when your vision becomes a reality and calculating what it will cost you not to get there will shoot adrenaline into your willpower to make it happen.

Why?

This question requires you to make clear why you want to do what you want to do. The answer you give to this question should be convincing and compelling enough to help you keep working towards your vision, even if it seems extremely demanding. You have to develop this desperation to fulfil your vision, which stems from the knowledge that the only reason you survived birth and your mother didn't have a miscarriage or a stillborn was for you to fulfil this vision. Until you come up with your own compelling reasons, I will allow you to adopt this reason. I find it compelling enough. If you were born to fulfil this vision, then you better do it, or else you will have wasted your existence.

Different people have different reasons for wanting to pursue their visions. For some, it may be personal reasons; setting visions and achieving them makes them tick. It's what gives their lives meaning and a reason to keep living. For some, it's a spiritual reason. They believe God placed them on earth for a purpose, and this purpose is summarised in their vision. They feel that not fulfilling the vision will make them feel like they have failed God. Still, some are tired of the life they have been living, and they have decided to come up with a vision to help them improve their lives. Whatever your reason, just make sure it is strong enough to compel you to keep moving even when you feel discouraged and find it tough to go on.

When?

Setting timeless goals is a recipe for failure. Napoleon Hill said, "Goals are dreams with a deadline." Your goals should be time-bound. That will help keep you focused and working diligently, knowing that you do not have forever to work on those goals. Don't just sit there and say, "One day I want to do this; some day I want to go there." Be specific about the time. Just say next year this time I will have done this and that. Terry Savelle-Foy said, "Someday is not a day in the week. It doesn't go like Someday, Monday, Tuesday, Wednesday..." Once you say someday and leave it at that, you won't feel pressured to act because every other day will still be someday.

Asking yourself the "when" question helps you approximate the time by which you want to have your goals accomplished. It gives you a deadline to work against and helps you formulate a timeline you can follow to keep yourself on course.

Where?

Depending on the nature of your goals, this question may be answered with a physical location or otherwise. If you feel your dream cannot be well achieved in your home area, town, or even country, don't be afraid to spread your wings to wherever your vision will flourish. It is a fact that not all places have the capacity to handle your vision. But there's definitely a place somewhere in God's vast earth where your dream will know no limits. Search for that place until you find it. Don't be afraid to relocate if you have to, even if it means leaving your comfort zone—your place or country of birth. I dare you to do it.

Your vision may be bigger than some places, and if you insist on living in those places, you will find that it becomes suffocated and never sees the light of day.

How?

This is one question that is not always necessary to answer. In some cases, depending on your goal, trying to answer this question may make you despair and lose hope in achieving your dream, especially if you can't come up with a satisfactory answer. I personally have been a victim of this. My dreams seemed too big and resource-intensive; I just couldn't figure out *how* I could secure the resources I needed to get started.

But, in some cases, answering this question may give you more clarity and direction. For example, if your goal is to come out of debt, the "how" of this goal would be to avoid using your credit card or even destroying it. It can also involve saving a percentage of your income towards settling your debt.

If finding a satisfactory answer to the "how" question seems impossible, don't stress too much. That doesn't mean your dreams and vision are out of this world and impossible to achieve. Referring to Prov. 16:1, the preparations of the heart belong to man, but the answer of the tongue is from the Lord.

Now, what does this mean? "To man belong the plans of the heart." This simply means it is your responsibility to have a plan for anything that pertains to your life. Don't be lazy and expect God or someone else to do it on your behalf. It is *your* responsibility! As it has been said, if you fail to plan, you are planning to fail.

Then, the second part says, "But from the Lord comes the reply of the tongue." What reply? You ask. I mean the reply to the question that's been bugging you, "How will my vision happen?" This reply from the Lord carries an answer to how these plans you have made will be executed and financed. If you don't have any plans, then you won't get this reply. The "how" part of your vision is none of your business and all of God's business. The planning part is none of God's business, but it's all of your business. That's the deal! God and you are in this together. The main and important thing is for both parties to keep their end of the deal. Only then will the vision become a reality. There are no doubts or questions about that.

It had always been a dream of mine to study abroad. I asked myself, "*How* will I get there?" "How and where will I get the funding?" But that was really none of my business, but God's responsibility to supply all my needs according to riches in glory, as He promises in His Word. Mine was to dream of studying abroad and plan what course I would like to take when the opportunity comes. I did that. It took many years before this dream became a reality. That doesn't matter; what matters is that the reply from the Lord eventually came. I got a very good scholarship, and I pursued my dream as planned.

God is always true and faithful to do His part. If your vision is not happening or seems to be failing, it's not His fault, but yours. If you don't give God a plan, you give Him nothing to work with. Remember, God's provision is for a vision. He cannot be giving you any sort of provision if you don't have a clearly spelled-out plan for how you will utilise the provision. Where the purpose of a thing is not known, abuse becomes inevitable. If you don't have a plan for how you will use God's provision, you are most likely to abuse it.

After you have broken down your vision into goals, it will be easier for you to start working towards it. Sometimes your goals may take as little as a week (short-term) or as long as 5 years (long-term) to start taking shape. In this case, it becomes necessary to further break them down into daily objectives. Dissect the broad goals and refine them into simpler objectives that you can work on daily. When you do this, you will discover that it becomes even easier and more exciting to work on your vision. This will further make it easier for you to make your life what you want it to be. All you are trying to do here is ensure that working on your dream or vision is not stressful. So, keep breaking it down to the simplest components possible—small bites that you can swallow without choking.

Vision ➜ goals (long and short term) ➜ daily objectives

Now, just in case you are wondering why it is important to go through the process of coming up with goals and daily objectives, the reason it is this important and a step you cannot overlook if you really intend to see what you envision happen is because goal setting helps you come up with a map for your life—a plan. The goals may initially be independent of each other, but you need to harmonise and organize them into a plan. You can organise your goals by sequence, that is, in the order you want to achieve them. You can also organise them by priority—what is more important and urgent versus what is less important and can be attended to later. This will give you a sense of direction and help you be organised and able to take control of your future.

Set dynamic goals. Don't set goals that will make you hit a dead end once accomplished. Let your goals be flexible enough to evolve with you as you achieve them. Let your goals change as you get closer to your vision, broadening each time.

Consider this example. Let me say you dream of having a tuck shop by the roadside where you sell grilled meat to people who pass by. That tuck shop is a good start, but it shouldn't be your end goal. After you set it up and it's up and running, allow it to evolve into a more formal restaurant. The restaurant will now offer even more options on the menu. More options mean more income.

Once the restaurant is fully functional and you have mastered its operations, allow it to evolve into more restaurants in different towns. Let it become a chain store that will serve a wider population. The evolution of this goal can go on and on.

By now, I know you are probably thinking this is easier said than done. But I also know we can both agree that it is not impossible to do. Adopt this adage: *"The difficult things we do immediately; the impossible may take some time."* It may not be easy, but it's doable, and you can do it. Just adopt this example of allowing your vision to evolve for your specific goal and see how it works for you.

Now, let's look at a few things that planning can do for you.

Your plan will protect you.

Sometimes doing good is the enemy of doing what is right. Doing good can actually keep you from doing what is right. Your plan will protect you from doing what is good at the expense of what is right. What is right is what contributes to making your vision a reality. This is where all your energy should be focused. "Good" is not always "right", depending on where your vision directs you. There may be some good people around you which are not right for you as you design your life. These people may drain you and reduce your productivity, sucking up your time and energy. Some good people will suck up your energy. They will be busy telling you why you can't achieve your vision, contaminating you with self-doubt and fear.

Fear is a subtle result of a deep-seated feeling of inadequacy. It is just a display of your conditioning, not your potential. It has absolutely nothing to do with what you are capable of doing (your potential), but it has everything to do with what your mind has been made to believe, either by experience or by the people around you. The kind of conditioning that breeds fear is conditioning with the wrong information. The right people will tell you why you are well able to achieve your vision. They will offer advice on how you can go about doing it, cheer you on, and get you all fired up to reach for it.

Your plan will protect you from people who are "vision quenchers" ensuring that you keep pursuing your vision with minimal problems.

Your plan will help you apply purpose to your time

Ever heard someone say, "I am killing time."? You can't afford to kill something you desperately need. Time is what life is made of. If you "kill" time, you are indirectly killing your life.

The reason some people have time to kill is because they don't have a plan for their lives. Without a plan, you have no purpose for spending your time. You just spend it however you want. Planning helps you determine ahead of time how you will be using the time on your hands. If you are on a mission to design your life, every second counts. You don't have time to waste. You have to be able to account at the end of each day for how you spent the 24 hours in your day. How you use that time depends on your purpose and your plan.

If you fail to assign your time to a specific purpose, you are giving other people the power to control how you spend your time. If, for example, you are home lying idle, then your friend stops by and invites you over for drinks. You are likely to jump at the idea because your friend has just come up with a plan for your time. You can't live like that if you are serious about working on your vision. You cannot afford to be tossed to and fro by other people's suggestions on how to spend your time. Until you have a solid plan for your time, this is unavoidable.

Planning for today helps you take control of your future .

You can possibly know with certainty what the future holds for you based on your plans for today. Whether you succeed or fail in the future, it all depends on the plan you have or don't have today. The future will not be a surprise because it doesn't just happen. What you are today is the sum of what you have been doing in the days before today. If you don't like what you look like today, then today is the best day to start taking control of your future. The starting point is planning. You invent your future with a plan today. The vision you have for your life is in the future. It marks the finish line. Planning allows you to hit the finish line before you even start.

To summarise everything, planning helps keep you on track until you hit the bull's eye—your vision. According to Dr. Myles Munroe, "Planning is the management of the distance between conception and destination; it is the management of the distance between breath and death."

Having neatly and clearly laid out your plan and goals, the next step is to carry out that plan, i.e., put it into action. After all the time and energy spent on coming up with those goals and objectives, it will all go to waste if you don't stand up and act accordingly. Don't get tired of seeing this; Dr. Myles said, "Planning without action is futile, and action without planning is fatal." I totally agree with this statement. Don't you?

6

Do it afraid!

Coming up with a vision for your life may be easy. Setting goals to help focus your efforts towards achieving your vision may seem like a daunting task, but you can still handle it. Breaking down those goals into objectives that you can achieve one at a time may be equally challenging. It requires the same strength as coming up with your goals. But you can most likely also handle it without a problem. You know why? Because all this you do in your personal space, and no one knows about it unless they hear from you.

Putting your goals and objectives into action is a different story. Because now, this demands that you leave the comfort zone of your privacy. People around you may get to see what you are trying to do; it's no longer your little secret. There are risks involved here, including the risk of failure. Now, failure is associated with a stigma. It brings with it a plethora of feelings, including humiliation, embarrassment, and feeling inadequate, among others. Many people who can't stand these feelings are crippled by fear. In the midst of that fear, don't ask, "What if I fail?" or "What if it doesn't turn out the way I anticipate it to?" Rather ask, "What if it all works out fine?" That may ease a great deal of the tension.

Fear will cause you to miss opportunities that would otherwise mark a turning point in your life. It will erect some walls right in front of you to block the path on which you are travelling. It's important, however, that you do not merely see walls before you but see the doors in the walls. If one particular door closes, hold your peace; don't panic, because another one will open sooner than you think. If you allow fear to hold you hostage, you may not get to where you want to be.

Once you have the vision and goals clearly written down, don't allow the fear of failure and the humiliation associated with it to counteract the thought of getting started on charting your course towards your desired destiny. In the event failure hits you hard and sends you crashing on the floor, make sure you bounce back like a tennis ball and not break like an egg.

Many of the successful people out there began their journey to success in fear. The difference with them is that they did not allow their fear of failure to cripple them and hold them hostage. They were courageous enough to forge on despite the fear. Courage will not remove fear from you, but it will enable you to consider the attempt to fulfil your vision more important than the possible humiliation in the event you fail. Courage doesn't deny or ignore the possibility of failure. Instead, it helps change your perception of it. It refuses to let you see failure as a monster that you can't reckon with. It helps you accept any possible failure in your pursuit as a learning curve. Every successful person looks for something positive in every failure and always finds it. This is what keeps them going. Otherwise, failure would cripple them.

As a matter of fact, Brian Tracy says, "There is no failure, just feedback." Some of the feedback may not be pleasant; that's the problem. Courage enables you to realise that failure is not final; it doesn't mean you have hit rock bottom. It is just feedback that tells you that you used the wrong method for whatever you were doing. Feedback makes you better, smarter, and wiser, no matter how unpleasant it may be. Instead of despairing in the event you fail, just take time to look for and find the right method, then keep going. Courage, persistence, and endurance are antidotes for failure.

Winston Churchill once said, "Courage is the ability to go from failure to failure without losing enthusiasm." Do not allow failure or setbacks to steal your enthusiasm. View any setback that you can ever come across as a set-up for a comeback. After every seeming failure or setback, instead of losing your enthusiasm and excitement for designing your life, brace yourself for a "celebrity style" comeback. Even if you were knocked down, get up, shake off the dust, square up your shoulders, wear your broadest smile, and keep going. There is no reason to feel sorry or ashamed about it. Why should you?

Look at it through Thomas Edison's eyes. Faced with failure, he says, "I have not failed; I just have found 10, 000 ways that won't work." This should be your attitude towards failure. After a setback, celebrate that you have just discovered one of the methods that does not work in this case. Refine and modify it, and keep going. Your assignment is to keep looking for that method that actually works until you find it. Diligently guard against the loss of your enthusiasm while at it.

You have to adopt a childlike mentality. When a child learns to walk, no matter how many times she falls or how hard she falls, she won't stop trying until she can walk without stumbling and falling anymore. For a child, learning to walk is not an option. She eventually needs to know how to walk. Don't make the fulfilment of your vision optional; make it non-negotiable. Don't just be interested in your vision; be committed to it. If you are only interested, you will only do what is convenient and comfortable to do. But if you are committed, you will do whatever it takes, no matter what. Tell yourself that you will do it even if it's the last thing to do before you die. Don't stop working on your vision until you get it right.

I enjoy listening to stories of successful people because I am interested in knowing how they got where they are. I have noticed one thing that is almost common in each of their stories. Each of them, when they tell their stories, has some kind of failure that pops up.

Donald Trump, America's former president, is a very successful businessman. He too, when he tells his story, mentions failure at some point in his business ventures. He says he once lost billions of dollars in an investment gone wrong. I am almost certain that no one can be truly successful without having experienced some kind of setback at some point in their lives. I am not saying it is impossible. It is possible, and that much I cannot dispute. There are a number of people who haven't experienced failure in their lives. All I am saying is that the people who experience failure are more than those who just sail through without any challenges. So, in the event you find yourself having to gaze at failure, don't quit and think you are the only one. Many people have been down this path before you, but they didn't quit. Why should you? What distinguishes successful and unsuccessful people is how they perceive the failure they face.

You don't fail because you are dumb, incapable, or cursed. You fail just because you missed something in your method. Your responsibility after a failure or setback is to identify the thing that you didn't do right and correct it. Don't expect fear to go away before you can start acting on your vision; that will not happen. It is actually when you start working that you will discover that there was nothing to fear right from the beginning. Your fears were unfounded.

I remember when I wrote my first book. Writing a book had always been my dream. Fear engulfed me. I asked myself a lot of questions. "Who knows me?" "Who will be excited to buy my book?" "Will there be anyone interested in my book at all?" "What if no one buys my book?" "How will I cover the publishing costs?" The more I asked such questions, the deeper I sank into the mud of crippling fear.

It wasn't until after that that I had realised that asking these questions was doing me more harm than good. I stopped, took a deep breath, built my courage, and kept writing. I finished my book, published it, and got it out there. People were happy to buy it. I should have known right from the onset that there was nothing to fear. Because of my unfounded fear, I wasted precious time. Had I overcome that fear early enough, who knows? Maybe I would have published my tenth book already.

Fear can be a good thing, though. Fear sometimes becomes necessary to keep you on your toes and moving towards your dream. Can you imagine a student who is not afraid of failing? He won't spend time studying and won't bother writing and submitting assignments on time. He becomes negligent. The one who is afraid of failure involves himself and studies for extended hours. He makes it his responsibility to seek clarification where he doesn't understand. His fear of failure keeps him on his toes and on track.

Your fear may also be important to keep you on track towards your vision. If you are afraid of failing, you will make sure that you seek all the help you can get as you design your life. You will find yourself surrounded by role models and mentors—people who have walked the path you are walking and successfully reached their desired destination—the same destination you are aspiring to reach. Identify those people, associate with them, and ask them as many questions as necessary to give you a clear direction to keep forging your way. Take advantage of and use the wisdom they have acquired through their experience.

Truly successful people will not hold back answers to questions that will help you design your life and succeed. Guess why? Because where they are, there aren't many people, and it tends to be lonely. If they see someone who is interested in joining them, they get excited because it means more company for them. So, believe me when I say there is nothing to fear. Keep working towards your vision, even if you are afraid. Use the fear to inspire you to work hard so that you do not become one of its victims.

7

Get yourself mentors

You have to realise that what you call your "dream"—that very thing you hope to achieve in your lifetime—is someone else's reality. Someone out there is living your dream. It is, therefore, your responsibility to search for that person and find him. Brian Tracy says success leaves tracks. Look for a person whose achievements you admire, and have that person as your mentor. Watch this individual closely, look at the tracks behind him, and then follow them diligently. If you are lucky, it can be someone within your reach—maybe someone in your country or even your hometown. In that case, you can have the luxury of requesting a meet-up with that individual and relay to him your story. Find out if he will be willing to help you navigate through life until you get to where he is and subsequently get to your vision.

A mentor is someone you can look up to, ask them questions without shame or intimidation, and be free to interact with them. Get close to that person. As you spend time with them, you will absorb their winning attitude, energy, world view, and behaviour. The more time you spend with them, the more you become like them. Make sure you choose your mentors carefully. Not everyone qualifies to be your mentor. Your vision will dictate to you the qualities that you have to look for in a mentor. Your mentor should be the embodiment of your dream. He should be your dream personified—someone who is several steps ahead of you.

Sometimes you might need to go online to find a person who qualifies as your mentor. In such instances, it might not be possible to meet them face-to-face. But thank God for technology and social media. You can follow that person online, read their blog posts, read their books if they have any, visit their websites, and all that. Don't worry, this is not the same as stalking. Just do anything to get a sneak peek at what makes them tick. So, if your dream is to play professional tennis like Serena Williams, build a multibillion dollar company like Bill Gates, be the queen of gospel music like South Africa's Rebecca Malope, or do anything at all, then you need to spend time studying the lives of those who have already done what you are trying to do.

The truth of the matter is that your vision is unique to you, and as such, it is not likely to find a person who has the exact same vision or all the components of it. That is why, sometimes, it may be necessary for you to have several mentors. From each of them, identify special qualities that you admire. Study how they achieved what they have achieved. Learn from each of them as much as you can, and allow them to inspire and provoke you towards your dream. Learn from their mistakes and make it a point not to repeat them.

Do not allow the inspiration from your role models and mentors to stop at just fascinating you. Act on them while you are still inspired. Inspiration that is not promptly taken advantage of will soon vanish. Brendon Francis Brown once said, "Inspirations never go in for long engagements; they demand immediate marriage to action." How true! That is why, after you are inspired, you need to act promptly. Use your inspiration as fuel to propel you towards your vision while it lasts. Allow it to launch you and get you started on the course towards your dream. Just like a bow launches an arrow, allow your inspiration to launch you towards fulfilling your dream.

There is this principle that many people overlook and thus find themselves losing out in one way or another. The principle says, *"what you don't use, you lose."* Worded differently, it says, "Use it or lose it." The principle is irrevocable and holds true in many aspects of life, including inspiration and motivation. These two feelings are not permanent. They are aroused by certain events for only a short period of time. After that, they slowly fade away and eventually die a natural death. A wise person knows this and uses it to his or her advantage.

Inspiration and motivation are necessary to get you started. But, because they are short-lived, they are not sufficient on their own to keep you going until you get to the end. Your passion does that. It takes over where inspiration dies off, just so you keep going. You owe it to yourself to be passionate about your dreams if they will eventually come true. Passion is the glue that helps you stick to your dream until it materialises.

Passion gives you staying power. It births in you that determination that refuses to give up, no matter how bumpy the road to your dream becomes. It helps you perceive any obstacle as a stepping stone instead of a stumbling block and any setback as a set-up for a comeback. Determination and passion give you a fighter's spirit that will turn any breakdown into a breakthrough. It gives you that tenacity of a bulldog, which says I won't give up until I achieve what I set out to do.

In the pursuit of your dream, there will be times when you want to give up. The reasons for giving up may be valid, but your passion will not allow you to. It will cause you to forge your way until you get there. At this time, you will be very lucky if you still have your inspiration and motivation. These are not meant to sustain you through the journey; they are meant to kick-start you. Your passion is what sustains you.

After you have achieved your vision, despite the hardship you went through and withstood, celebrate yourself. As I said earlier, what gets celebrated gets repeated. Celebration is like a reset button. It sets you out on the journey once again. After achieving one dream, dream again, then set out to achieve it once more. I guarantee that when you go for it the second time, the vision or dream will be much bigger and consequently more demanding. But, having achieved the first one, you will have built up enough courage to take it on. Your vision-accomplishing muscles will have been fully exercised and ready for action. As such, you shouldn't struggle like you did on your first attempt. Do not cut the cycle; never stop dreaming. The accomplishment of one dream should mark the birth of another. As long as you live, there should never be a point in time when you stop having a vision for your life. The day you stop should be the day you breathe your last. As you achieve one vision, the next should be greater than the first; that's how you will advance in life.

A common mistake that many frequently make regarding mentors and role models is to copy and imitate them. This is a big mistake. It will suffocate you and kill your dream. Role models and mentors are not there to be mimicked or imitated. They are there as "templates" to help give you an idea of what the finished product should look like. If you imitate someone, you make life monotonous and boring. You live a life that has already been lived by someone else. You deprive the world of the original and unique you. If you are ever tempted to do that, just know that you have limited yourself.

If you are imitating someone else, no matter how hard you work, the best you can ever be is second-best. The person you are copying will always be the best. But if you just remain who you are, then there are no limits to what or who you can become. Learn from your mentors, but live out your own life, maintaining your authenticity. Be original and be yourself, because an original is always worth more than a copy. If you end up imitating your mentors, you limit yourself, and you will never know how amazing you can be.

Getting yourself mentors and role models is very important. Rub shoulders with them and spend time with them. Watch closely to see how they do things and learn their language. Study how they deal with failures and setbacks; observe how they plan their day and let it roll out. When you do all these things, you will find out what makes them different from the rest. Successful people do things that other people are not willing to do. They also don't do things that other people do. Your assignment is to find out what those things are and apply them in your own life. Keep company with successful people, and you will soon add to their number. Remember, birds of the same feather flock together.

A little advice that you can add to your mentor selection criteria: consider choosing those people who had very little or nothing when they first began but were still able to get where they are—where you want to be. From these people, you can learn how they overcame the obstacles that arose when they first started off. How they transitioned through all the intermediate stages until they finally became the people you envy today. Minimise those people who were born into it.

If your dream is to start a business, avoid following people who inherited their businesses from their families, or anyone else for that matter. There is not much they can teach you about starting a business. The best they can give you are tips on maintaining an existing business. They were not there when it started, so they are not likely to give you sound advice on starting up. If they do, they will only offer you secondhand information. Find a person who can give you first-hand information. He will be a better and more reliable source of the information you need because he has the capacity to outline step-by-step how he got to where he is.

8

Use the gift of creative imagination

When God created us, He endowed us with numerous gifts and treasures that help us live and enjoy our lives to the fullest. Not to undermine all the other gifts, but to me, the best gift in life, other than life itself, is the gift of imagination. This gift allows you to enjoy living in the future while still being in the present. Harness the power of your imagination to frame your world. Take advantage of the fact that God created your brain to think in images. Use that to see the completed picture of your destiny.

The book of Ephesians 3:20 (NKJV) says,

> *"Now to Him who is able to do exceedingly abundantly above all that I ask or <u>think</u>...,"*

Another version, the NIV, says it slightly differently:

> *"Now to Him who is able to do immeasurably more than all I ask or <u>imagine</u>...,"*

We have been given a priceless gift: the gift of imagination. We think and imagine with the mind that God has given us. The verse says God exceeds our thoughts or imaginations in His actions. So, the question is, if we haven't imagined anything, what will God exceed? If we haven't thought about anything, what will God exceed?

Imagination helps you reach places that your physical body may not reach. Imagination helps you conceive brilliant ideas that may even be unique to you. Once conceived, the ideas in your imagination may burn like fire in your soul and yell to be birthed. At this time, be very cautious about who you associate with and who you share what you imagine with.

Look for people who have conceived just like you. When you meet those people, the baby (your idea) will leap for joy. That is, the drive to birth your idea will become stronger. By this you will know you have met the right person. If, after meeting and talking to a particular person, you begin to think your idea is ridiculous and lose the drive to birth it, then hanging around that person for longer will be detrimental to your vision. Such a feeling is a good indicator that the two of you are incompatible and not cut out of the same material. You know what they say: "iron sharpens iron." Such a person cannot add any value to you. Instead, they may cause you to miscarry that which you are trying to birth—your vision.

You will know you have met the right person if, after the meeting, you become energised to push through hindrances and barriers, overthrow walls, and skip over traps until you realise what you have always envisioned in your imagination. Be careful of fire quenchers. Those are the people who will talk you out of what you have imagined and give you reasons why you can't have what you envisioned. If you give them your attention and listen to them long enough, suddenly, what they are saying will start to make sense to you. The moment that happens, there goes your dream—down the drain. If you don't see what they are saying to you as deception, then deceit will creep in and cause you to abort or miscarry what you imagined.

I will liken your mind to a womb. It incubates what you imagine until it comes to fruition. Just like a baby that is born prematurely has reduced chances of survival, the same is true for your vision or what you imagine. You don't have to hasten to "give birth" or to execute it. Wait patiently for it. Give it time. This is the time you have to use for setting your goals and coming up with objectives. The gestation period of your conceived dream ends when these are clearly spelled out and in place. That is the only time that your dream is mature and ready to be given birth to. Until then, keep it in your "womb" and continue incubating it. Once born and out there for everyone to see, the product of your imagination will be called your "brain child." This is actually proof that your brain has a "womb."

This I know for sure: no mind is barren and incapable of conceiving. But until a mind is inseminated with imagination, an idea, or a vision, it will not produce a brainchild. Some people are either scared or too lazy to push and give birth the normal way. They would rather opt for adopting another person's brainchild. This means they use another person's idea and do not even modify it to make it a new version that belongs to them. This is what is called "re-inventing the wheel." It absolutely undermines the intelligence of the person who is copying someone else's idea, and it's an insult to his creativity. Don't undermine or insult yourself like that. If you do that, you are only limiting yourself, and it does you no good. Allow your creative imagination to soar as high as it wants. If possible, even reaching heights that no one has ever tapped into, thus bringing you unheard of ideas. Nurture your mind with great thoughts, and then a great life will be your nature.

Just like everything else under the sun, the mind can be abused. If you don't understand the purpose that God had in mind when He gave you your mind, you are definitely going to use it in all the wrong ways. Each time you use anything, whatever it is, for what it was not meant for, you minimise the chances of that thing being used for its purpose.

Your mind is supposed to be used more for imagination than for memory. Imagination focuses on the future, where the vision for your life is, while memory focuses on the past. If you spend most of your time memorising the past—the struggles you probably went through, the people that hurt you, the opportunities you lost, and all such painful and energy-draining memories—you are draining your mind of the energy that it is supposed to use in the imagination process. You also don't leave it with enough time to do the imagination.

Your past is in the past; that's where it belongs, and that's where you have to leave it. Don't drag it into your future. The past does not have the power or the ability to hold you back because it is not where you are. But remembrance of the past is potent enough to hold you back and keep you from moving forward.

The only thing that you are allowed to drag from your past into your present and future are the lessons you learned from it—those lessons that you consider vital for your future. It is only those lessons, and nothing else. With regards to the relationship between the past and the future, I agree with Yadira Panto, who once said, "Although the past is the sculptor of the future, the love of the future is the eraser of the past." Considering this truth, no matter what kind of pain and heartache are in your past, you owe it to yourself to love your future so much that the past and everything in it become immaterial.

I strongly discourage people from failing to use the gift of imagination to frame their future. But then, let's say, for some valid reason, you are not able to do it. The least you can do is realise that the present moment (because you are so shortsighted you are unable to see beyond today) is all you have to make your life. Then, focus on it. Leave the past exactly where it is.

Having successfully engaged your mind in creative imagination, conceived the idea, nurtured it, and laid out a plan to avoid its premature birth, the next step is action. Now, this action is not supposed to be just random.

Imagination is one of the simplest things in the world, especially because it doesn't require physical strength. Action is not as easy, as I have already mentioned. It is a little more demanding because now it involves physical energy. But the most difficult thing when designing your life is aligning your imagination with your actions. Until you act in accordance with what you have imagined, then your imagination is in vain.

I believe by now you see how important action is in designing your life. It is irreplaceable and unavoidable. That is why I mentioned at the beginning of the book that you have to be an active participant in your own life. Don't just be a passive onlooker who observes what happens to him. Make life happen. Every point that I have discussed thus far ends with action.

Now, no matter how busy your life is, take some time out and just sit still and think hard. Imagine what you want your life to look like in the not-so-distant future. Just be still and use your creative imagination to take you wherever it so desires. Lao Tzu said, "To the mind that is still, the whole universe surrenders." If you take time to imagine, your life will eventually turn out beautifully, and you will be no ordinary young person.

9

Be an utmost person

Pastor Paula White once taught about three groups of people that exist today. The "almost," the "most", and the "utmost" people. Which category you fall into is not by design, coincidence, or mistake. Belonging to any one of these categories is by choice. Some people make this choice consciously, while others do it unconsciously. Consciously because, although they know that there is another place they could possibly be, they are not willing to do the things that will take them there. They are just lazy. They have learned to be comfortable with the status quo and are not ready for change. As you might know, change is one of the most dreaded things in the world. John Asaraff once said, "The only human being that likes change is a baby with a wet diaper." Change can be very scary because it disrupts the usual and alters what has always been.

To be able to move towards change, you first have to be uncomfortable with the status quo and the way things have always been. Look at where you would rather be and compare it to where you are. Then, decide if taking that leap will be worth it. You are not going to move from where you are until you see where you would rather be and consider it a better place. This demands that you have what I call foresight—the ability to see what lies ahead before you even get there. It's similar to the imagination we just discussed. Many people lack this ability; they have become so accustomed to their current circumstances that they can no longer see anywhere beyond them. You are not ready to be an "utmost" person if this defines you.

Whether you made a conscious or unconscious choice to affiliate with any of the groups, the fact is that you are personally responsible for it. You cannot blame your circumstances, background, or the people around you. If there is anyone to blame at all, it's you. Do not see anything that you are as a disadvantage or a hindrance to becoming a better you.

Your background does not have the power to keep you from achieving what you set your mind to, unless, of course, you allow it to. There is no law that stipulates that people from a background like yours aren't supposed to achieve greatness and live in abundance. So don't blame your background, or anything for that matter. I have never seen anyone who plays the blame game achieve much in this world. Blaming another person for your circumstances is tantamount to throwing yourself a pity party. Your guests will comfort you and make you comfortable right where you are. You will then see no reason to get moving. The blame game is one of those things that wastes your energy. The very same energy you could be using in to design and improve your life is the same energy you waste pointing fingers. Don't do that.

Back to the groups, the "almost" group is made of the people who set out to do something, then because of some reason leave it uncompleted. When they talk about what happened you will hear them say, "I *almost* passed this class.", "I *almost* qualified for varsity.", I *almost* started the business.", I *almost* did this and I *almost* did that. This obviously shows that the individual didn't make it good. Maybe he quit at the verge of the victory or just missed the mark altogether. Whatever the case, my advice to such people would be, don't stop trying until you succeed. You cannot afford to quit. You know what they say, quitters never win and winners never quit. Don't join the quitters, you should hang in there until you get there. Whether what you are aiming at is your vision or just anything in life.

The "most" people. These are the people who find comfort in the crowd. They don't want to do anything that will make them stand out. *Most* teenagers start engaging in sexual activities while still in high school. "So, if everyone is doing it, why shouldn't I?" They ask. My answer would be, "Because you are not everyone, but just you." Don't do things just because everyone else is doing them. Do things that you consider to resonate with you. *Most* people do not have a vision for their lives. Then, why should I be the odd man out? As long as you are comfortable doing what everyone else is doing, you are never going to realise your full potential, and you will always be just another ordinary person. With this attitude, you will join the *most* people who exist. You shouldn't just exist, but live. Live your life the best you know how. Live your life in such a way that, on your death bed, you will have no regrets about wasted opportunities. Les Brown once said, "The thing about life is that you can't come out of it alive. So, do yourself a favour, live it to the fullest, and enjoy it." You really can't enjoy life, or live it to the fullest as long as you are comfortable being a part of the *most* group of people.

The last group is my favourite. I choose to join this group. The "utmost" group is made of people who break norms and challenge the status quo. While the members of the *most* group are trampling over each other at the floor and the ceiling limits the *almost* people, the *utmost* people break the ceiling and draw the breath of fresh air above it. The floor is crowded, everyone is there. There is a stampede and lots of people will be stepping on your toes. Just go a little bit higher and break the ceiling. Be comfortable with doing things that *most* people wouldn't do. Take those risks, ask those questions, and make those sacrifices. I dare you to be different, don't try to fit in with everyone else. Be a trailblazer, a trendsetter and keep going. *Utmost* people do not go where there is a path. They break new ground, going where there is no path and leaving a trail for other people to follow.

I know many people will come up with reasons why they can't live the *utmost* life. "I am not educated enough." "I don't have talent." "I don't have money." This may all be true. I am not even going to attempt dismissing it. I know of many people who got good education and created a better life for themselves. I also know of several other people who struggled in school, dropped-out but they followed their talent and made a fortune. But again, this much I know with certainty, to achieve great things in life and join the *utmost* people; talent doesn't matter, education doesn't count, how little or how much money you have is also immaterial. The only things that you can't do without are passion and determination. These two are must haves before you even start off.

If you have education, talent, or money in addition to passion and determination, that's nice. Passion and determination will enable you to keep at whatever you are pursuing no matter how demanding the journey becomes. They are going to build enough stamina to propel you forward. Quitters don't have these. Good news, these qualities are not sold anywhere nor are they hereditary. If they were, some people would be in the unfortunate bloodlines without them and have reasons to justify themselves. These two can be developed by anyone within themselves if they will.

Whatever the landscape of your life looks like currently, I strongly believe you have all it takes to design your utmost life. I believe in you even if you don't believe in yourself yet. Zig Ziglar once said, "A lot of people have gone further than they thought they could because someone else thought they could." I think and believe you can. So, even if you think you can't, just hang onto what I think and believe about you and watch how things will turn out.

To be an *utmost* person, sometimes it is necessary and would help if you become blissfully ignorant of some things. In such cases, ignorance is bliss. So many things in this life are possible as long as you don't know that they are impossible. When it comes to things you can't do or achieve in your life, choose to be ignorant. Once you consider some things possible and others impossible, then you have limited yourself when it comes to what you can or can't do. Towards those things you have considered impossible you will have crippled energies and contracted ability and thus for you, they will definitely be impossible. It will be surprising; however, how other people still manage to do them if indeed they are impossible. I believe there are no limits to what you can do with your life, as long as you set your mind and heart to it and have the passion and determination to do it.

Ignorance to what is impossible is nicely demonstrated by a bumblebee. I once read of a study that was conducted by an aeronautical engineer on the bumblebee. This study found that the surface area of a bumblebee's wings and the force that the bee's muscles can generate are too small to lift its weight. Its body was considered to be too large to be supported on its little and feeble wings. In light of these findings, the laws of aerodynamics state that the bumblebee should not be able to fly. But, have you seen a bumblebee before? Because it is ignorant of the scientifically calculated limitations, the bumblebee flies without any problem and reaches for the heights. Because of its ignorance, it is able to achieve what scientists consider impossible for it and accomplishes what the experts do not expect of it. These calculations assume that the bumblebee will use flight mechanisms that resemble those of a plane. But why should a bumblebee fly like an aircraft because it doesn't even look like it in the first place?

Based on some things that characterise your life: the kind of neighbourhood you grew up in, the school you attended, the grades you obtained through out your school years, and many other such things. Based on these, logic may tell you that you can't achieve much in life. A life of abundance is not possible for you. People may even give you examples of other people with similar experiences as yours and how they fared in life. The truth is, you are not those people. Your story is unique and it's not going to be dictated by someone else's.

Just like the bumblebee, choose to be ignorant of all those calculations made about your life. Keep flying and see if you are not going to soar up into the sky. Choose ignorance and achieve what seems impossible. Chart your own course, don't expect to achieve your dreams the same way other people achieve theirs. Their methods may not work for you. It is highly possible that the bumblebee would indeed not fly had it attempted to fly like an aeroplane. But it flies so well in its own way, harnessing its uniqueness.

Unlike the bumblebee's limitation which were just a myth, sometimes the limitations can be real; and actually affect you as you try to reach for the life you have always dreamt of. Still, these limitations being real should not be a reason to despair or quit. There is always a way around limitations. To demonstrate this, I will use a penguin.

A penguin is a bird with black and white feathers. Like all other birds, it is supposed to fly. However, due to its physical limitations, which are real, a penguin is not able to fly. In spite of these limitations, the penguin didn't just give up and accept that it can't fly. Instead, it evolved and adapted. If you have seen a penguin before, you must have noted that although it is a bird, its wings, feet, feathers, and beak are not like those of every other bird. This is because while most other birds are built for flight, the penguin, because of its limitations evolved in readiness not for flight up in the air but for 'flight under water'. They are said to reach a speed of 35km/hr. when they swim. Now, why would a penguin make a fuss about flying in the air if it can still 'fly' under water this good? Who, in the whole wide world, in their right frame of mind, would stress about flying if swimming can bring the same result? The penguin is able to reach any place it wants to through swimming, just like the 'normal' birds reach any place through flying. Albert Einstein, the popular scientist said, "Everyone is a genius, but if you judge a fish by its ability to climb a tree, it will spend its whole life believing it is stupid."

The penguin represents the times when the experts are right about your limitations. If you can't get to your dream through the path you had initially anticipated, then change and adapt. Re-strategize! Don't just sit there, sulk and whine, accepting failure. That will not get you anywhere. Instead, take what you have and figure out how to make it work in ways that will make your calculated limitations meaningless. Once you are clear that your attempt to your original intent to fly is not working, don't despair. Just be happy that you have just discovered a way that doesn't work for you and thus you are not going to waste any more time and energy trying to make it work. It is better to do something and fail or make a mistake than to do nothing flawlessly.

In your pursuit of being an utmost person, be ready to embrace the challenges, change the norms, break paradigms, and transcend the limitations and constraints perceived by others.

As an utmost person, you compare yourself to yourself. I have observed over the years that human happiness is related not only to how much a person has or has achieved. But rather what he has or has achieved relative to others. This is one mindset that has prevented people from being happy with who they are and what they have accomplished in their lives.

People are always looking over the fence. What does my neighbour have? Where does she buy her clothes? Don't do that to yourself. Don't stoop that low to making another person the benchmark of your success. The only person you are allowed and actually, expected to compete and compare against is yourself. Look at where you were yesterday, compare it to where you are today. Assess whether you are making any progress at all or just moving in circles. Your life will improve if you constantly pause to reflect about your progress. This should be your daily habit. Before going to bed each night, make sure you reflect on your day. How productive were you? What did you accomplish? What is still outstanding?

Your benchmark or point of reference should be your vision, not someone else. You can have people you look up to but not with a mindset of competition but to draw inspiration from. At the end of the day, your vision or your dream should be the utmost model to orient and inspire you. Your goals, which are basically your vision broken down or simplified should serve as a yardstick to help measure how far you have come and how close you are to hitting the bull's eye. Compete with yourself, not with your neighbours. If you are not happy with where you are today, decide not to be in the same place tomorrow. That will keep you moving forward and help you improve constantly.

10

Sometimes you win, sometimes you learn

....

I know what you're thinking already. You are probably thinking the title of this chapter should have been; "Sometimes you win, sometimes you lose." But that's quite obvious, isn't it? So, why don't we just put a positive twist on the way we view our not-so-pleasant experiences? We can do that if we look at our seeming losses as learning opportunities.

Don't allow your losses or failures to define who you are. Keep your losses outside of your being, because that's where they belong. Never ever describe yourself using your negative experiences. Perspective is key. That is, how you see yourself in the face of an unbecoming situation matters. Almost everyone experiences some kind of loss in their lifetime. Such is life. Of course, the magnitude of the losses varies. Some may be insignificant, and others may be very significant. Regardless of its magnitude, no loss is desirable.

Personally, I don't like losing anything, not even a pen. A pen doesn't even cost much.

So, since losses are inevitable in this life, and unfortunately, each individual will likely experience quite a number of losses in their lifetime, it would be better, therefore, if we dared to change our perception of loss. Instead of viewing loss as a loss that strips us of the satisfaction and pride that come with winning, why don't we change and look at loss as an opportunity to learn? When you lose, just know that you just learned a way that doesn't work. Learn something of value in the process—something that will make you wiser so that your next attempt will be more informed.

Make sure you don't waste your lesson. Use it to help others who you see are doing what doesn't work. This attitude will help you not become shadowed by failure. It will help you hang onto a strong, positive sense of self. You will know that just because you haven't realised what you set out to do yet, that doesn't make you a failure. A failure would be an individual who loses interest in trying again once things don't go the way they would have preferred them to. If you are willing to try again, then you are not a failure.

That's the attitude you have to adopt at all times. Don't be discouraged or disillusioned when things don't go the way you would have preferred them to. Always keep a positive attitude. If you win, be happy and celebrate the best you know how. If things don't turn out your way, be happy and find out what might have gone wrong. Compile the lessons to be learned from the experience and work on them. No outcome should be wasted. All outcomes are either worth celebrating or learning from. If you adopt such an attitude, then you will win at life all the time, no matter what comes your way. Such is the mindset of many of those people you admire and look up to. Do you want to join their ranks? Then do what they do and think like they think.

Find a reason to be happy, always! It will be medicine for your soul. Sadness and a gloomy countenance are crippling. Refuse to allow your circumstances to dictate how you feel on any given day. Make happiness a goal each day when your feet hit the ground in the morning. I know this doesn't come easy, which is why you have to make it a daily decision until it becomes a habit that's part of you. Do it until happiness comes naturally to you. Just be happy in spite of everything. Not everyone who is happy has their life all figured out and running smoothly like a well-oiled machine. You will be surprised at how topsy-turvy the lives of some of the happiest people are.

As it has been said, refuse to look like what you have been through or are going through. If you spend today as a happy person, it will help you to be able to look forward to tomorrow not only with great anticipation and enthusiasm but also with the positive energy you need to make things happen that day. The starting point for making every day count is to begin the day with sufficient energy, and that energy is easily generated when you are happy. Sadness is energy-draining and paralysing. It stifles your productivity and creative imagination, rendering you ineffective in most of the activities you will be engaged in during the day.

Having said all this, one should never downsize the pain that comes with not winning. Loss and failure hurt a lot! But when you are hurting because of a loss or failure, just know that some of the most valuable lessons we need to make us better people come wrapped up and packaged as failures. Make sure you unwrap the packaging and draw out your lesson.

11

You don't have time to waste

"Dost thou love life? Then don't squander time. For that's the stuff life is made of."

Benjamin Franklin

"The future started yesterday, and we are already late."

John Legend

We have come a long way. From the beginning of the book to this last chapter, I have shared with you insights that, if you give them attention and practice them, they will dramatically transform your life. The fact that you kept reading until this very last chapter tells me a lot about your determination to design your life. For this reason, I want to encourage you to get started right away and waste no more time. You really do not have any more time. You are already late because the future started yesterday.

Franklin, in our opening quote, asked this important question. "Do you love life?" Responding to this question without giving it much thought is easy. But you don't have to respond to it in words. If you respond in the affirmative, then you will stand to your feet and right away start practising the suggestions I make in this book. Dissenting will be shown by maintaining the status quo in terms of how you have been doing things and how you live your life.

Your future comes one day at a time. How you spend even a single day of your life has implications for your future. Be intentional and purposeful in the way you spend your days, redeeming your time and making the very best out of it. Make sure that you recognise and take advantage of each opportunity that presents itself to you; use it diligently and with the utmost wisdom. You don't have forever to make your dreams a reality.

Don't wait for perfect conditions before you can start pursuing your dreams; you may find yourself waiting for a lifetime and never getting anything done. Perfect conditions do not exist. You will find that you are always missing at least one or two elements to have what you consider perfect conditions. That's not a problem, and it should by no means stop you from pursuing your dream. You don't really need perfect conditions anyway. If you hope someday will bring you what you consider to be perfect conditions, then you are likely going to wait for your entire lifetime and never get started. Remember Terri's saying? "Someday is not one of the days in a week."

Sometimes the path to your purpose may be so winding that you feel like it is just a long road leading nowhere. I know this because I've been there. You know the point where you feel like you are going nowhere and just moving in circles? At times, you may know exactly what you should be doing, and your purpose may be clear to you, but you just don't seem to know where to start with the pursuit. In other instances, you may know where to start but not have the courage to begin. At other times, you may have the courage but not the resources. Rarely will the variables you need for the pursuit of your purpose line up the way you would like them to. Rarely will you have perfect conditions that will make you comfortable enough to step out and pursue what you believe is your purpose. Many of the people who are living out their purpose today will tell you that they started out afraid, and they were not even sure they were doing the right thing.

Have you ever wondered why other people's lives are so productive? One would swear that some people have days with 26 hours. Yet still, for some other people, a day ends and they have literally nothing to show for it. You would swear that they skipped some hours of the day. The reason for this is quite simple. The first group of people are aware that they don't have the whole time in the universe to make life happen. They understand the saying, "Time and tide wait for no man." They are intentional about their lives and they refuse to live by default. You know the default settings of life? You wake up in the morning, take a bath, have your breakfast, go to school or work, have your lunch, return to class or work, go home, have dinner, go to bed, and wake up the next morning. The cycle continues for 365 days, and you complete a year. You start the next 365 days, and your life follows the same pattern repeatedly.

Everyone is dealt an equal amount of time in a single day— 24 hours. What makes the distinction between the two groups of people is not their geographical location or family background. Rather, it's how they spend those 24 hours in their hands that determines what an individual accomplishes in a single day, building up over a lifetime.

In this day and age where almost everything has been automated, we have machines designed to help us with our daily chores, from cooking and washing dishes to cleaning the house and all other activities. You would expect that we have more time to be productive. We have microwave ovens that cook food in minutes instead of conventional ovens that take hours and require constant monitoring. We have dishwashers in the kitchen and washing machines to do our laundry. All these are designed to save us both time and energy so that we can re-channel these two non-renewable resources to the most important things in life: designing our lives and pursuing our dreams.

This is not usually the case, though. Why? Because while we have these time-saving tools in one hand, on the other hand we have time-wasters like television sets where people watch useless things that do not add any value to their lives all day. We have cell phones that make us waste a lot of precious time on social media. I am not implying that you should be antisocial while designing your life. I am only appealing to your time management skills. While you use your time to catch-up with the world around you, make it a point that you assign some of this time to important things like designing your life. Balance up your time. Work hard but also play hard. Remember, *all work and no play makes Jack a dull boy*. That's not what I advocate for here. Do keep the quote at the beginning of this chapter at the back of your mind, though; if you really love life, you are not going to squander time.

The worst mistake that you can make now is to procrastinate and hope for someday to come before you start applying what you have learned in this book. Don't wait for those two days; they are not part of the days in a week, and they never come. You are sure of one day in your life, and that's today. That's the best day to start. Make it your primary focus. Decide that from today onwards, when your feet hit the ground each morning, your attitude will be that of a person who is not only ready to make a living but should be that of one ready to make a life.

You only have one chance at life; don't spend it making a living, but making life. You know what they say: tomorrow is the most appealing day to a lazy person. Don't make that true for you. You will never regain the time you keep losing. You only have one chance at life. You waste it; that's the end of the story. Don't wait for a perfect moment; the present moment is the perfect one; make it good. If you do that, I guarantee you that the rest of your days will be the best of your days.

With that said, I leave the ball in your court. It has been my absolute pleasure to have been with you through this book. Now, get moving, design your life, and experience abundance.

Maximum respect,

Hlelolwenkhosi